TOTALLY HAUNTED USA

WILLIAMSBURG, VIRGINIA

BONNIE GEYER FLOREK

ISBN-13: 978-1499518757
ISBN- 10: 1499518757

TOTALLY HAUNTED USA WILLIAMSBURG, VIRGINIA

A SPECIAL THANK YOU

To Quade Parker

Thank you for this beautiful cover. Your fine work never

ceases to amaze me. I do not believe there is any artistic medium that

you do not excel in. I am most appreciative of your fine work and

tireless cooperation. May success follow you wherever you go.

Bonnie Geyer Florek

CONTENTS

About The Book   vi
Introduction   vii

1. History of Williamsburg   1
2. Author's Personal Ghostly Experiences   7
3. Ghostly Tales of Guests and Employees   12
4. Bruton Parish Church   16
5. Graveyard   19
6. Public Hospital   21
7. George Wythe House   23
8. McKenzie Apothecary   29
9. Governor's Palace   31
10. Thomas Everard House   34
11. James Geddy House   37
12. Peyton Randolph House   38
13. Magazine   45
14. Mary Stith House   47
15. Wetherburn's Tavern   49
16. Brickhouse Tavern   51
17. Peruke Maker   53
18. King's Arms Tavern   55
19. Shield's Tavern   57
20. Palmer House   58
21. Capitol   60
22. Secretary's Office / Jones Graveyard   63
23. Public Gaol (Jail)   65
24. Pasteur and Galt Apothecary   68
25. Raleigh Tavern   70
26. James Craig Silversmith   73
27. Prentis Store   74
28. Tayloe House   75
29. Ludwell-Paradise House   78
30. Coke-Garrett House   80
31. Courthouse / Pillory and Stock   82
32. Matthew Whaley School   84

33.   The Ghost of Catherine Rathell   89
34.   The Ghost of Lucy Ludwell   91
About the Author   92
About Spooks and Legends Haunted Tours, LLC   93
Thank You to Fred Vick   95
New Tour Characters   96
Tour Sightings   97
Trip Advisor Reviews   100

About the Book

The first in a series, Bonnie Geyer Florek brings you Totally
Haunted USA

Williamsburg, Virginia is believed to be one of the most haunted
towns in America. Some people believe in ghosts, some do not. There
have been many skeptics who have become believers after attending a
Spooks and Legends Haunted Tour, however.

Ghosts have been seen and heard by guests and the presence of
spirits have often been felt. Just one visit to the Peyton Randolph
House has made believers of previous skeptics. A determined knocking
is often heard coming from the inside of the front door. The doorknob
rattles loudly and persistently as guests stand listening to true stories
originating from within those very walls. And what about the side door
slamming shut so hard that it makes you jump back a few steps? These
are just some of the goings on in town.....sights that can be seen and
sounds that resonate within your mind, long after you have returned
home.

The George Wythe House is no exception where haunts are
concerned. Just stare at those windows and see the inside shutters
open and close before your very eyes, though no one is inside the
house. No living soul, that is.

These are only a few of the many ghostly experiences
encountered in the town of Williamsburg. To hear of more excitement,
read on and then come and visit us for a one of a kind, ghostly tour.
You will never forget nor will you want your ghost-loving friends to
miss this. Enjoy!

*Read Bonnie's other series, Totally Haunted UK, based on researched
ghost stories of England.

Introduction

Williamsburg was Virginia's capital from 1699-1780. Starting as a small settlement it grew to be the size of a small city.

By the mid-1700s the population of the town was close to two thousand, of which half were slaves.

When court was in session the population of the town more than doubled. People of the Virginia Colony traveled into town to enjoy governor's balls, fairs and 'Publick Times.' Townspeople and guests dressed in their finest just to stroll the streets, impressing others with their finery. The children enjoyed the fairs, most especially playing 'Pig with the Tail Soaped.'

The beginning of America's democracy and liberty started here in the 1700s. The Colonists began questioning British rule. Taxation was opposed by Patrick Henry, wanting representation in the House of Burgesses. In 1774, the First Continental Congress was presided over by Peyton Randolph. George Mason wrote the Declaration of Rights which later became the first ten amendments to the Constitution. Housed in Williamsburg were thousands of Continental Army soldiers. By 1780, Thomas Jefferson thought Richmond better suited as Virginia's capitol city. Williamsburg was then no longer a town of social, political and economic standings. Though it remained the county seat, it was mainly a town for area farmers to market their goods.

The Public Hospital and the College of William and Mary were all that remained of importance in town. The wealthy no longer resided in Williamsburg, which contributed to the deterioration of the homes and buildings. Some even burned, though fortunately most homes and buildings continued to be used. Had wealth remained in town, original 18th century structures would have been removed or altered beyond restoration to accommodate the growth of the capitol city.

In 1923, W.A. R. Goodwin, the rector of the Bruton Parish Church, had a vision to restore the town to its 18th century appearance. He lacked funds for all but the restoration of the church. After meeting John D. Rockefeller, Jr. in 1926, Goodwin invited him to visit Williamsburg at which time he shared his vision with Mr. Rockefeller. He agreed to anonymously fund the restoration, first purchasing the Ludwell Paradise House for just $8,000. In order to remain anonymous, Mr. Rockefeller signed all documents as 'David's Father.' When townspeople became concerned about the anonymity of the purchaser, the plan to restore the town was finally revealed. As restoration began to take place, townspeople who had initially opposed it realized the economic benefits. Most residents were allowed to remain in their homes through tenancy agreements until death. At first, Mr. Rockefeller had little intention of funding the entire restoration, though his enthusiasm grew as research unfolded. Drawings, maps and records were found in American and European libraries as many historic details emerged.

Much attention was paid to architectural detail as teams worked to reconstruct and authentically restore original 18th century sites. The more modern buildings were removed or razed whenever possible. Today, the town looks very much as it did in the 18th century. It is said there would be little noticeable difference to Patrick Henry or Thomas Jefferson if they walked the streets today.

Roughly one million guests visit the town each year. This historic living history museum houses hundreds of restored public buildings, residences, outbuildings, dependencies, shops, and hotels, plus acres of formal and informal gardens, pastures and walks.

1. History of Williamsburg

1606-1926

1606--- 105 British settlers sailed to Virginia on the Susan Constant, Discovery and Godspeed. Called the Virginia Company of London, their primary motive was profit. 145 came, one died, 144 arrived. 105 were settlers and the rest were sailors and officers.

1607---144 settlers arrived at Jamestown Island which was named for James the First. It was the first English speaking settlement in America.

1619--- The first representative government was formed as well as the first capital of Virginia. One hundred women arrived and slavery began.

For 90 years, it was the wealthiest, largest of 13 colonies. The area did not fit the image.

1699--- The statehouse had burned four times, there were many mosquitoes, brackish water, and safety issues. The Capitol moved onto higher, safer ground which was then called Middle Plantation, between the York and James Rivers. It was later renamed Williamsburg for King William III.

Francis Nicholson designed the city. He had also designed Annapolis when he was the governor there. He named 2 streets after himself in both towns. Owners had to purchase ½ acre lots, build on them within 2 years, erect a fence around each lot, and all buildings had to be the same distance from the street. Duke of Gloucester Street, the main road, was ninety-nine feet wide and 1 mile in length. The city was anchored on 3 principles, the Capitol representing law, the College representing education and the Church representing religion.

General Court met in Williamsburg each year in April and October for a two-week period. The Court of Oyer and Terminer (hear and decide) met in June and December. These two courts met in Williamsburg for periods called 'publick times.'

When court was in session, leaders such as Thomas Jefferson and Patrick Henry were present and vendors poured into Williamsburg to sell their wares. There were grand balls and parties. Everyone wore their finest clothing, even if just to parade down the streets. Taverns and lodging houses were filled with burgesses and other travelers. Williamsburg was exciting.

Those who lived in town were of many different classes. Two percent of the population were of gentry status. They lived in homes comparable to the Governor's Palace, having several outbuildings. The gentry were independently wealthy and did not have to work. They had many slaves to care for them and their household, and were scholarly plantation owners with great influence. The middling sort were farmers, craftsmen and artisans who lived in a home similar to James Geddy's. They would perhaps have an apprentice and a few slaves. The lesser sort was the lower class. They were unskilled workers who lived in a tenement house. The sub-class was made up of slaves and indentured servants who lived together on their master's property.

Once the Revolutionary War broke out, things dramatically changed in Williamsburg. Politicians who sided with England were forced to resign. Some citizens left town and fled to England for their safety. Some prominent families were torn apart forever because they disagreed on independence from England ie. John Randolph (Tory) and his brother Peyton Randolph (Patriot)

In 1775 Lord Dunmore, the governor of Williamsburg, made Dunmore's Proclamation. It called for marshall law (military), allegiance to the king and The Ethiopian Regiment. It offered freedom to slaves and indentured servants who belonged to Patriots, if they ran away to join the English army. Many were killed. Less than 2% ran, which were mostly women. They ended up in Newfoundland aka New Fin Land (Canada) and were treated like second class citizens.

When the general assembly decided to move Virginia's capital to Richmond in 1780, property values decreased and the town's population declined.

In 1781 Lord Cornwallis's English troops invaded Williamsburg. For several days they burned homes, looted stores, and took whatever they wanted. Cornwallis's troops pulled out of Williamsburg on July 4th and Lafayette and his troops entered the town soon after. In October the Battle of Yorktown ended British rule. Although the war was over, Williamsburg witnessed the horrors of battle as wounded soldiers flooded the town. Private homes, public buildings and the campus of the College of William and Mary were all turned into makeshift hospitals.

After the Revolutionary War ended, Williamsburg became a quiet, tranquil town. A person could walk half the length of Duke of Gloucester Street without seeing another human being.   Cows, chickens and goats roamed freely on the dusty roads. This peaceful setting ended during the Civil War.

By the 1800s the city had become run-down. There were still 88 original 18th and early 19th century buildings standing when Rev. W.A.R. Goodwin came to Williamsburg as rector of Bruton Parish Church in 1903. This inspired him to restore Williamsburg.

In 1926 Rev. Goodwin enticed John D. Rockefeller, Jr. to financially back the restoration of the city. After decades of planning and reconstruction Williamsburg regained its 18th Century grandeur. Today there are 88 original buildings, 350 total buildings, 301 acres of land, and 7 ½ miles of fencing. All buildings are owned by the Colonial Williamsburg Foundation except for one, the Bowden Armistead House. It is of Civil War era and its architecture is Greek Revival.

Inportant Dates:
1609-1610-Starving Time
1614---John Rolfe discovers tobacco and marries Pocahontas
1622---Indian uprising along the James River
1624---Virginia becomes a royal colony

1693—James Blair persuades William and Mary to charter the College. It is the 2nd
            oldest college in America, the first being Harvard (1636); Christopher Wren—
                  court architect

1704---Assembly moves to new capitol building, completed in 1705; Gaol (jail) built

1747—Capitol Burns---rebuilt and burns again in 1832.

1763---French and Indian War ends (7 Year War)

1764---Sugar Act (tax)

1765---Stamp Act. Patrick Henry gives Caesar Brutus Speech

1766---Stamp Act Repealed; Declaratory Act passed---England could tax Americans
            whatever they wanted as they are in control of the colony

1767---Townsend Acts---tax on paper, paint, lead, glass, tea

1769—Virgina boycotts purchase of British goods; Lord Botetourt dissolves the Assembly
/ House of Burgesses and again in 1774 when they vote for a day of fasting, humiliation
and prayer

1770---Townsend Acts repealed except tea; Boston Massacre, Courthouse built

1773—Boston Tea Party, Public Hospital opens per Governor Fauquier

1774---Boston Harbor closes, 1ˢᵗ Continental Congress meets, Burgesses vote for
fasting, humiliation and prayer; Dunmore dissolves assembly.

1775---Battles of Lexington and Concord 'Shot heard around the world.' Second Continental
Congress meets; Gun powder is stolen by the British; Governor Dunmore and his family flees.

1776---May 15ᵗʰ –Virginia declares independence; June 12ᵗʰ –Virginia adopts the Declaration of
Rights (written by George Mason), later becomes the Bill of Rights; July 4ᵗʰ –
Colonies declare independence; July 6ᵗʰ –Patrick Henry becomes the first commonwealth governor and Phi Beta Kappa is founded

1778---France enters the war as an American ally

1780---Capital moves to Richmond to be less vulnerable to attack. Thomas Jefferson is governor

1783---Treaty of Paris; War is over; Britain recognizes the USA

1861-1865---Civil War

1926—WAR Goodwin convinces John D. Rockefeller, Jr. to fund restoration of Williamsburg

1832—Capital burns for 2nd time.

1934---Franklin D. Roosevelt calls Duke of Gloucester St. 'the Most Historic Avenue in America.'
> The restored town opens to the public.

2. Author's Personal Ghostly Experience

I must admit that I was more than skeptical for quite a while, even after experiencing things that were happening to me, personally. After I first moved to Williamsburg in 2002, I went alone one evening to the historic area. I began taking photos as I had been told spirits would come alive late at night.

I knew nothing about where specific sightings or sounds had been seen or heard so I just randomly started taking photos. I had a film camera at the time, though many have since taken shots using a digital camera. It doesn't seem to matter which type of camera is used. The outcome is the same.

First I went to the Wythe (pronounced "with") House and took several photos of the upper right two windows. I kept clicking away not knowing of any logical reason to do such a thing. When I had the photos developed I noticed that each one showed the inside window shutters to be open to different widths between shots. I was so amazed. I could not stop thinking about it.

I happened to mention my findings to a town tour guide who assured me that my photos were not lying, that it was not my imagination. She said that those shutters always open and close. I was told to go back in the night time to see that the shutters would open and close before my eyes. Sure enough, she was correct. On my very next visit to the house I was able to stand and stare and see those shutters opening and shutting right there in front of me. Can you believe I still continued to be skeptical?

Not long after that time I was working for Colonial Williamsburg, walking guests to a few different locations to hear old legends. One of the stops was the Geddy House. My job was to take guests into the parlor and wait until they had heard a legend being told by a story teller. I knew that we would be there for at least 15 minutes so I thought I'd go upstairs, where I knew I could find a rest room.

I left the parlor and spoke with Will, who was standing in the center hall. He and I had worked together before so we knew each other well enough to share experiences. I told him I was going to go upstairs to the rest room and that I would be right down. I had only been upstairs in that house one other time in the day light, so I was hoping I remembered where the bathroom was located. Though I had a good idea of where I was heading I had no idea where any of the light switches were and never did find any. Fortunately however, the shadows from the candlelight below stairs were just bright enough to find my way.

Since it was very dark I was not unhappy to be heading back down the hall to the stairway, minutes later. I must admit that I was a bit uncomfortable in the dark, in that old creaky house. I started back down the stairs when I noticed Will staring up at me, leaning on the banister and watching for my return. The look on his face only solidified my own fears.

I asked what was wrong, sensing something in his expression. He said he had been listening for me while waiting for my return. He did not wish to alarm me before I went upstairs by telling me of his earlier experiences. Come to find out he had heard heavy footsteps walking the floor above, just minutes before I headed to the upper floor. Somehow I was not surprised, though I did not want to believe it. I had heard from others that the sound of heavy foots was not a rare occurrence in that house.

As if that were not enough, Will had more to tell me. He had experienced a frightening occurrence earlier that night. He arrived alone to set things up for the evening. Walking toward the front of the house, he happened to look to his left into the shop area. There, standing in plain sight was a black woman in 18th century clothing staring at him. The house had been closed up since 5 pm when he arrived around 7 pm. He smiled and said hello to the woman, though she did not look familiar to him. She did not respond. As a matter of fact there was no emotion on her face at all.

Will went no closer to the shop area, but kept his eye on the shop doorway, afraid to move. The woman just stared back at him, as she appeared to be straightening up the shop area in complete silence. Suddenly, he could no longer see her. He got his nerve up and walked into the shop area. To his surprise the woman was gone, despite not having heard the door open or close or any other sounds. Consequently, he vowed never to work there again.

Quite a while ago I was giving a tour standing on the green, across from the Peyton Randolph House. The group was made up of teenagers. They were a great group and very attentive. Suddenly however, there was a commotion I did not understand. They seemed not to be listening and were pointing off to my left. I stopped and turned around, knowing there was something there that was taking their attention. When I turned to look, there was a porch light going on and off as if someone was playing with the light switch. This was happening in the one-story area of the house where an old woman lived, as she still had a life-right to do so. The light finally stayed off and I ended the tour a while later. The very next day, I heard that the old woman had died right around the time we saw the light going on and off. Later on, I heard that the old lady used to flip the light switch on and off if the tours were being noisy. Funny thing is that we were the only group there and we were very quiet. I always wished I could have told the group about her death, but did not know how to contact them since I was working for another company at the time.

I used to walk the town before 7 am, a time when many walk in that peaceful and beautiful town. This particular morning was rather dark as the sun was just beginning to come up at the Capitol end of Duke of Gloucester Street. I was making my way around Palace Green and was heading toward the Wythe House when I saw one of the shutters partially opened in the front left room. There in the window was a woman in 18th century clothing wearing eyeglasses, standing there staring out at me. I knew no living being was in that house at that time of morning. I looked over at the woman and smiled, nodding my head. She did not look familiar to me. There were no other costumed interpreters in town yet, for the day. They do not arrive for work until around 8:30 am. As I walked past the house I continued to look at her. I noticed that this woman was practically staring through me, yet had no expression on her face. As I continued to watch her she suddenly vanished before my eyes. Later on I found out that the house was not even open that day.

Even those experiences did not cure me of skepticism. What did cure me, however, is the Peyton Randolph House. It has quite a dark reputation. Some say it is the most haunted house in Williamsburg, others say it is the most haunted house in all of Virginia, while still others believe it to be the most haunted house in the entire United States.

There have been many nights when I have been standing in front of that house, along with my tour groups. With my back to it, it can get rather frightening when guests who are staring at the house begin to whisper, gasp, and have the look of fear on their faces. In such situations, I have been known to run right through the group to get away quickly.

The front door knob often jiggles, continuing for quite a while. When this happens, the security guards show up within minutes to see if anyone is trying to enter the house. There is an alarm that goes off which the guards admit happens often in that particular location.

While out giving a tour one night, the side door opened and slammed shut so loudly that it was heard all the way down to the other end of town. The whole group screamed. Because I was not facing the house as the group was, I ran the other way as quickly as I could. I had no idea what was happening behind me. I stopped the tour then and there just to spend time watching and investigating further.

Not long ago, another situation arose. Again, I was giving the tour when I kept hearing things like 'Oh my gosh!', 'What is that?', and 'I'm leaving!' coming from the group. I quickly came out of character, as I turned around and saw apparitions in the windows. There was one apparition walking behind the three lower left windows as we watched, and another looking in from outside. As we continued to look we could see what seemed to be a little child reaching up to hold onto the window sill, peering out from inside the house. We all stood there in shock for quite a while.

With all I have experienced, and all I have been told by those who work or live in the historic area, I am finally a firm believer that historic Williamsburg is full of ghosts and haunts.

3. Ghostly Tales of Guests and Employees

Some of the town security staff are quick to share stories and personal experiences. One such security guard, who often visits with tour   guests,   tells   of   his   ghostly   encounters. He is quick to show a bent key that was used to not only get into the Peyton Randolph house but also to try to get back out of the house. The man who used the key, on one dark night, went inside to take care of things. When he went to leave, he put the key in the door and began turning it. He turned and turned for quite some time. The door did not unlock, but the key bent. Tour guests are often shown that very same bent key.

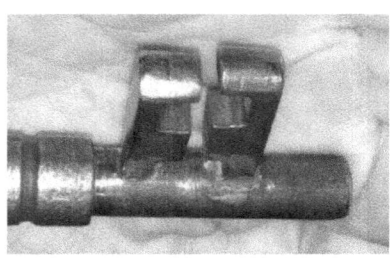

The security guard also tells of the eeriness in the George Wythe House. Though many feel the Peyton Randolph House is the most haunted, this particular security guard begs to differ. He says that he can feel other spirits in that house late at night. He has seen apparitions walking the floors while odd sounds are heard.

One of the employees in town was working at Wetherburn's Tavern. She was there alone in the early morning. When she walked into the large dining room she felt very uncomfortable. Suddenly she felt her tied back long hair being pulled. She turned only to see the hair elastic fall to the floor. She vowed never again to be in that house alone.

One morning in the Peyton Randolph House, one of the employees went in to start her day. A few other people had arrived before she got there. A lady who often worked there was standing on the landing of the beautiful staircase. The employee looked up and greeted her. As the day went on, she never saw the woman again. She mentioned to the other workers that she was looking for the lady who had earlier been on the staircase. They told her that she could not have seen her, as she had died early that morning.

One night while working for another tour company, I was standing outside the Kings Arms Tavern waiting for a group who was going to tour with me. A woman who saw my lantern came over and asked if I were leading a ghost tour. When I told her yes she began to speak, though she did seem a bit apprehensive. She asked me if I believed in ghosts. Quite honestly, at that time I was a bit skeptical, though I had seen and heard them many times. When I said that I believed, she told me that she hoped I was not going to think she was crazy, but she had something she needed to tell me.

She and her husband had visited before and stayed in the hotel facility at the Quarter. It is a very small accommodation right near the Inn, on the corner. It was originally a slaves' quarter centuries ago. She said that when they stayed there it was in the winter time and she had been pregnant. In the middle of the night, they both suddenly woke up and felt ice cold, though they had gone to bed with a heavy comforter over them. When they put the light on, not only were there no covers on them at all, the comforter and sheets were rolled in a ball over in the corner of the room. Needless to say, they did not sleep very well the rest of the night.

The Quarter

I recently received a photo from a guest who had gone on our tour. They had visited the Governor's Palace during the day. They wondered if I could explain the ghost of a child sitting in one of the chairs, in the photo. I had no idea who it was, let alone why she was there, but it was clearly a ghost.

Ghost Girl in the Governor's Palace

4. Bruton Parish Church
Corner of Duke of Gloucester Street and Palace Green

Bruton Parish Church was named after a town in Somerset, England on the Brue River. A national landmark, this original building has been in continuous use since 1715. Anyone in the 18th century who was an English citizen was an Anglican of the Church of England, a state church. After the Revolution it became Episcopal.

The church was built in cruciform shape. The bricks were laid in Flemish bond style. Mr. Tarpley of Tarpley's store donated the bell in 1761. It was purchased from the same foundry in England as the Liberty Bell, in Philadelphia. The bell tower was built by Benjamin Powell, 'undertaker' (contractor) from town.

Inside the sanctuary, English box pews were used for warmth where hot bricks could be brought to keep church members' feet warm. The balcony in the back is where William and Mary college students sat. As a matter of fact, it is said that Thomas Jefferson carved his initials in the balcony railing. Professors of the college sat in the front balcony. The main church sat in hierarchy; gentry, middling sort, lesser sort, sub-class. The governor sat in his red cloth chair in the front and his 12 counsellors sat next to him.

The pulpit is wineglass shaped with a sounding board. The chancel in the front represents heaven and the nave represents the body or earth. The three plaques in the front of the church are the Ten Commandments, the Lord's Prayer and the Apostle's Creed. The baptismal font is from Jamestown. Bodies are still buried beneath the floor of the church, today. The last burial was by the altar and is the body of W.A.R. Goodwin, the rector responsible for the restoration of the town in 1926.

In the 18th century, taxes were paid to the church. You were expected to attend at least one Sunday a month or you were fined. These taxes were for the care of the poor.

Today there are 1400 members.

In 1765, Robert Nicolson and sixteen other men submitted a petition to York County Court. They wanted to receive permission for occasional worship at a place for Public Worship of God according to the Practice of Protestant Dissenters of the Presbyterian denominations. The court granted them permission to worship legally outside the Church of England though still obligated to pay taxes to support Bruton Parish Church. In 1776, the General Assembly suspended the requirement that dissenters separated from the Church of England pay parish taxes. The Presbyterian Meeting House is located behind the capitol building.

Presbyterian Meeting House

Some years later, two men by the names of Gowan Pamphlet and Moses started a church called the 'African Church.' It is now the 'First Baptist Church of Williamsburg.'

5. Graveyard
Corner of Duke of Gloucester Street and Palace Green

Williamsburg is a town of many dark secrets that our forefathers never revealed to anyone else. These secrets continue to live on not only in Williamsburg, but in many parts of Virginia and the entire world.

In America, it all started as far back as the arrival of Sir Walter Raleigh and the history of the Lost Colony.

From the time of our country's inception, secret societies were controlling our future as they planned for a nation much different than its inhabitants were led to believe.

Many people have tried secretly to dig in the graveyard over the years, looking for a hidden mystical vault that was supposedly buried secretly in colonial days. It is said that it contains copper cylinders holding the lost manuscripts of Sir Francis Bacon, a philosopher. Some believe these papers, buried in 1676, would hold the key for a 'new united world, and would be a precursor to the second coming of Jesus Christ.' Believers still feel that these manuscripts will prove that Bacon was actually the author of the great works that have been attributed to William Shakespeare. One dig got to the depth of 20 feet which found a box of about 10 feet square. It was clearly too wide to be a coffin. At that point, the church ordered the dig be stopped and the hole was filled.

In the graveyard are many bodies of people who were quite important at the time of their death. They were often from prominent families in the colony. One such gentry man is buried behind the church. His name is Daniel Parke Custis. He was Martha Washington's first husband before he died. She and Daniel had lost two boys who are buried above Mr. Custis. In the late night, if you go to the side of the graveyard and look through the gate, you very well may see the Washingtons standing there by the grave, spending time with Mr. Custis and the boys. As you watch they suddenly vanish before your eyes.

6. Public Hospital
Corner of Francis and South Henry Streets

On June 4th, 1770 the House of Burgesses passed a bill to establish the Public Hospital. This was the first public institution for the mentally ill built in Colonial America. Opened in 1773, and known as the 'Hospital for Lunaticks,' this facility first treated its inmates more like prisoners than patients. They were confined to small primitive cells and the devices used to treat patients were implements of torture.

From 1773 to 1835 it was part prison, part infirmary. Its first keeper, James Galt had formerly been in charge of the public gaol (jail). His wife Mary became the matron for the female patients.

Only persons considered dangerous or curable were admitted. To calm or cure patients during the 'Age of Restraint,' the staff applied mechanical restraints, prescribed potent drugs, employed the ducking chair or plunge bath, and used instruments to bleed them.

The 'Moral Management Era' from 1836 to 1862 saw a new approach to mental health care. Moral management de-emphasized restraints and stressed the importance of kindness in efforts to cure the mentally ill. Physical labor, organized leisure time activities, and careful medical supervision were also important aspects of everyday life. Patients were urged to participate in crafts, gardening, and musical diversions and to talk with one another and with the staff.

By 1859 the hospital housed three hundred patients in seven buildings. On June 7th, 1885 a fire of undetermined origin completely destroyed the 18th century building which was reconstructed by Colonial Williamsburg in 1985.

Today, the hospital is also the entrance to the DeWitt Wallace Decorative Arts Museum which is located beneath the reconstructed hospital.

7. George Wythe House
West Side of Palace Green next to the Grave Yard

This is an original home built in Georgian style. It is the most copied home in America and it shows what gracious living was in 18th century Williamsburg. The house boasts two large chimneys and a large central hall. George Washington used this house as his headquarters during the Battle of Yorktown.

A plantation in miniature, it was built by Mr. Taliaferro. It was given as a wedding gift to his daughter Elizabeth and husband George Wythe. Behind the house are symmetrical gardens, tree box topiary and an arbor of shady hornbeam. Outbuildings include a stable, smokehouse, laundry, kitchen and lumber house.

It is always surprising to realize how few people know of George Wythe today, having been one of the most famous men in the 18th century. He was the first law professor at the College of William and Mary where he taught law to Thomas Jefferson, James Monroe and John Marshall. He was admitted to the bar at the young age of 20 and influenced Thomas Jefferson more than any other man. He framed the Constitution, signed the Declaration of Independence, was the first lawyer and judge in America, and was the clerk of the House of Burgesses.

After the siege of Yorktown, the house accommodated dozens of wounded men who fell during the battle. A young French soldier named Colonel Oscar LaBlanc was one of these men. He was making a swift recovery when he suddenly took a turn for the worse. A local woman named Katherine Anderson watched over the sick officer night and day. She was completely dedicated to the dying man, spending every waking moment by his side. When Colonel LaBlanc was no longer in danger of dying, the couple made plans to marry. Katherine was very happy. Her love for the French hero grew stronger every day. Unfortunately, he contracted malaria from one of the other patients. As he grew sicker, Katherine continued to take very good care of him. This time she could not save him and he died just one week after contracting malaria. Her grief was unbearable and she lost the will to live. Soon after, she died of a broken heart. Tourists have heard voices and footsteps coming from the second floor for years. At night, shadowy figures walk the house's darkened hallways.

One man was working alone above stairs in the home when he heard someone call out his name. He didn't recognize the voice, but he was drawn to it. As he went toward the voice he saw the dark outline of a man standing in the hallway. He asked him what he wanted but he didn't answer. In front of his eyes, he dissolved into thin air. He no longer works alone in the Wythe house.

A guest of the house had a ghostly encounter as well. She was looking into one of the bedrooms on the 2nd floor when she saw a woman dressed in colonial clothing, standing quietly in the corner. She seemed upset. The guest turned to call to her sister but when she looked back, the woman was gone. There was no other door to lead out of the room except the one she was standing in front of. All that remained was the strong smell of antiseptic.

Though these broken hearted spirits are most certainly those of Katherine and the Colonel, there may be a happy ending to the otherwise sad story. They have reunited within this house, sharing love in death that fate stole from them in life.

Being a childless widower, Mr. Wythe (pronounced "with") wrote his will to his nephew, Mr. George Wythe Sweeney. He was a 'ne'er do well' who was impatiently awaiting his inheritance. He never worked a day in his life, and had no intentions of doing so. George Sweeney was known to drink too much, get in trouble with the law, gamble and steal from others, including his uncle.

Mr. Wythe was counting on his nephew growing to be a responsible man, so he granted his inheritance to him. However, Mr. Sweeney was gambling all the time and owed many men his financial losses. It came to pass that those he owed threatened him with his life if he did not pay what was due them. Of course, Mr. Sweeney had no intention of working to pay the debt. His uncle was the picture of health, even at nearly eighty years of age.

When George Sweeney realized how much money he owed and how hard he would have to work to pay it back, he knew there was only one way to get the money he needed. In the wee hours of the morning, he went to the kitchen outside of the house. He had a small white packet that he threw in the burning fireplace in the kitchen. It is quite possible that packet was from the arsenic he put in his uncle's tea that morning. After breakfast Mr. Wythe suffered from terrible stomach pain. He never left his death bed.

While awaiting the inevitable, freed slave Lydia Broadnax went to Mr. Wythe's bedside and told him of his nephew's odd behavior. Mr. Wythe had no doubt his nephew had poisoned him, as he had written some checks not long before that he had stolen from his uncle's desk. Mr. Wythe lived long enough to summons his lawyer to his bedside and change his will. Consequently, his nephew never got any inheritance.

Hardly able to speak, Mr. Wythe told his friends to have him cut open to reveal the truth, as he wanted Mr. Sweeney to pay for his terrible deed. His nephew did have his day in court. However, Mr. Wythe had helped to create a law years before that forbade a black person to testify against a white person in the court of law. Because of that law, the nephew literally got away with murder.

Miss Lydia later became short of sight, having also been poisoned by George Sweeney. Whether it was intentional or not, is not known. A few years later however, she wrote to Mr. Thomas Jefferson, telling him that she needed some glasses as her sight was so deteriorated. Mr. Jefferson was kind enough to pay for her to have glasses made.

Miss Lydia's spirit remains in Mr. Wythe's house, today. She is often seen standing on the front step of the house, looking down the road for Mr. Wythe's arrival, as she did so many times before his death.

Mr. Wythe is also often seen inside the house during day and night hours. Guests who enter the house see Mr. Wythe and Mr. Washington speaking with each other regarding the state of affairs in Yorktown. Mr. Washington used the house as his headquarters during the battle.

George Wythe was always very happy to welcome out-of-town guests to stay with him, while in town for important events. One such guest, Lady Ann Skipwith continues to haunt the house. She had come to Williamsburg back in the 18th century to attend a ball hosted by the governor of the colony. Her husband Peyton and sister Jean were also guests of Mr. Wythe.

On the night of the ball Lady Ann was dressed in a most exquisite gown. Of course, it was the latest of fashion from England as her husband was quite wealthy. She had her beautiful red hair pulled up and decorated with tiny pearls and ribbons. Along with her beaded gown, she wore red slippers on her feet.

Lady Ann was greeted by all the gentry awaiting her arrival, at the palace. As they escorted her in, her husband and sister were left behind and ignored. Of course, they were not attractive in the way that Lady Ann was nor did they have her personality.

The ball had not been going on for very long when Lady Ann ran from the palace, alone. Of course, that was something a lady never did. She expected all of her husband's attention that evening, as he was always very attentive. On this particular night however, Peyton completely ignored her. Instead, her sister Jean was the spotlight in his eye. He danced every dance with her, never speaking with Lady Ann or even looking in her direction. It was more than she could take.

Running down Palace Green she headed directly toward Mr. Wythe's house. While running, one of her little slippers dropped from her foot. She continued to run as fast as she could, finally making her way through the front door of the house. So very upset, she threw the door open with a force that caused it to hit the wall behind, making a loud, crashing sound. Of course the servants came running to the front hall, not expecting any visitors at that hour. The ball was not about to end for quite a while.

As they watched Lady Ann run up the stairs they knew something terrible had happened. Before they could speak however, Lady Ann was already throwing herself to the bottom of the stairs, where her body lay in silence. To this day, there is a black spot on that very floor where her body fell to its death.

That is not the worst part of that night however. Before her body even turned cold her husband married her sister Jean.

Lady Ann is often still seen and heard running above stairs at the stroke of midnight. Dressed in her beautiful ball gown she hopes for a different ending to that tragic night.

Guests today often have the opportunity to greet Lady Ann's ghost. Upon one of Williamsburg's security guard's suggestions, many go right up to the front door late at night. When they knock, they say 'Lady Ann I have found your slipper!' She is then heard running down the stairs to fetch it from them. She also often jiggles the door knob, trying to open the front door to personally greet guests.

While you are close to the house be sure to listen for the slamming doors, in the cellar. They are known to slam into the late night in the very cellar where the walls ooze with a clear liquid. No one can figure out what that liquid is, however.

Do not be surprised if while you are standing in front of the house you see the inside window shutters opening and closing ever so slightly, before your eyes. If you cannot see it clearly, be sure to take a couple photos of a window or two. When you get home, bring the pictures up close and compare them. You will realize that those shutters were indeed opening and closing before your eyes.

8. McKenzie Apothecary
West side of Palace Green

Dr. McKenzie was more than an apothecary or druggist. He also practiced as a doctor providing medical treatment, prescribing medicine, training apprentices, performing surgery and serving as a man-midwife. Dr. McKenzie made house calls to treat patients, concocted his own medications and trained apprentices. Some were also trained as surgeons.

Many of those same medications are used today ie.chalk for heartburn, calamine for skin irritations, cinchona bark for fevers, malaria and cardiac conditions.

Medical treatment was very expensive, as it is today. Consequently, townspeople often diagnosed and treated conditions themselves. Headaches were often treated by vinegar of roses, made of rose petals steeped in vinegar and applied to the area of the headache.

Apothecaries sold cooking spices, candles, salad oil, anchovies, toothbrushes, and tobacco, much like we find in our modern drugstores today.

29

Doctor McKenzie was an excellent doctor. He and another doctor from town worked closely together. Because they had worked so well together in life, they decided to also help each other in death. They wrote their wills together which stated that whichever one died first would leave the other his skeleton. Unfortunately for Dr. McKenzie he died first. Since that time his skeleton can be seen looking out the window of the apothecary.

A few years back a young man was on a Spooks and Legends Tour. At the end of the tour, he insisted on sharing a photo he had taken that night. There in the window of the McKenzie Apothecary was a skeleton, peering out. This had never been seen or noticed before that time. Since then however, many of our guests have been able to catch that same skeleton in their photos, though he has not been seen with the naked eye. Many have taken the good doctor home with them in their photos. He stands there in skeletal form looking out at his guests. His eye sockets often appear to house small red lights.

The Skeleton of Dr. McKenzie Looking Out the Window

9. Governor's Palace
At the North end of Palace Green

The most photographed view in America, this reconstruction sits at the north end of Palace Green. It is set on ten acres of land and boasts a beautiful entrance hall, ballroom, parlor, bed chambers, dining rooms, waiting areas and a wine cellar, the only remaining original part of the building. It is furnished from inventory of more than 12,000 items dating to the period of Lord Dunmore, Virginia's last royal governor.

The mansion was built over sixteen years' time between 1706-1722. Because of the length of time it took for the building to be completed, townspeople began calling it 'The Palace,' as they were paying taxes for its construction for so long.

In 1752 the rear wing was added as a great room for entertaining. The 2 heraldic figures on the gate are the lion (England) and unicorn (Scotland). There were seven Royal Governors who were the Commander in Chief, Head of the Armed Forces and the Head of the Anglican Church. They carried the full weight of the King's authority. The last governor, Lord Dunmore feared a Patriot attack and fled.

Two Commonwealth governors, Patrick Henry and Thomas Jefferson also made the palace their home. In 1780, the capital moved to Richmond, but the Palace was not empty for long. In late 1781 after the siege of Yorktown, it was used as a hospital for American soldiers and other critically injured victims who fought on the Patriot side. On December 22nd, 1781 the palace burned to the ground. It was not rebuilt until the restoration of Williamsburg in the late 1920s.

During the 18th century the Governor's Palace was the scene of many get-togethers of early America's elite. Dances were held about every three months in the Palace ballroom, each lasting up to eighteen hours, since many visitors had traveled 3 or more days on horseback to reach Williamsburg. It would have been terribly impolite to send them home too soon.

On the Palace grounds there is a stable and carriage house, a kitchen, scullery, laundry, and a hexagonal 'bagnio' or bathhouse, a real luxury in colonial times. There are beautiful formal gardens out back as well as a boxwood maze. Having burned, the Palace was rebuilt and opened to the public in 1934.

While being reconstructed in the 1930s, archaeologists found 156 men's and 2 women's skeletons in the gardens. These male bodies belonged to patients who had been treated at the Palace when it was a hospital. The women's bodies were those of the two nurses who cared for them. Among the bodies were musket balls with deeply imbedded teeth marks. Because there was little anesthesia, the wounded soldiers would bite down on lead balls during amputation to distract them from pain and to keep them from biting off their tongues. This is where the term 'biting the bullet' came from. Less than half who had amputations survived. Most died from blood loss, shock or infection. The bodies remain on that property today in the same mass grave where they were found.

The nurses' spirits have never left the property. Late at night, an inexplicable flickering light can be seen passing from window to window on the third floor. It appears that the nurses are still trying to care for the ill soldiers.

One night not long ago, a security guard went into the Palace alone. He was standing at the foot of the beautiful staircase that leads to the second floor. He stopped there, as he heard heavy footsteps walking toward him from the back room of the Palace. As the sound of the footsteps got closer he expected to see someone at any moment. However, the sound went right past him and up the stairs. There was no one in sight. Listening to the footsteps as they reached the second floor, they suddenly faded away.

As townspeople walk the streets at night they often see an 18th century servant up in the cupola, seemingly lighting a candle. Soldiers' screams can still be heard in the late night. They are the same screams heard during those very painful amputations centuries ago.

Many question how ghosts can be in a reconstructed building. Since ghosts haunt spaces and not places, they remain in the same space where they were long ago. This is why ghosts of old are often heard and seen in new houses which were built where tragedy once took place.

Not long ago, a visitor of the Palace took a picture of the hall way, directly in front of the entrance way. There was no one there. When they later looked at their picture, however, there was a young girl sitting on a chair in 18th century dress.

10. Thomas Everard House
East side on Palace Green

The Thomas Everard House is known for its fine carved woodwork. The yard is paved with original bricks found during excavation and the smokehouse and kitchen are original restored structures. This house was built by John Brush and occupied by Henry Cary, who extensively renovated it between 1730 and 1740. Thomas Everard moved into the house around 1770 and added wallpaper in the dining room and chamber. An immigrant from England, he served as mayor of Williamsburg two times, while supporting his family and nineteen slaves.

Mr. Everard was orphaned in England. He came to Virginia to apprentice in the 1730s when he was just a young boy. He was such a nice young lad that everyone in town liked him, most especially the slaves he worked with.

When he reached maturity he met a wonderful gentry woman. As was customary he inherited her wealth and properties through marriage. He was very good to his slaves and never separated them from their families, as many other masters often did. He could have become gentry, but he did not choose to.

In the course of his life, he was the Clerk of York County Court and was also on the vestry of the Bruton Parish Church.

Mr. Everard and his wife were very happy together and brought two adorable little girls into the world. They were always such sweet little girls, though they suffered great tragedy. At a young age, their mother became very ill and died suddenly. Though most single fathers would have put someone in charge of their motherless children's care, Mr. Everard chose to raise them without help.

Not only did he do a fine job, the girls grew to be wonderful young ladies. The elder daughter married into a nice family and remained in the colony. She and her husband later had children and always seemed to be very happy.

His younger daughter, Miss Frances decided she would move to England to find a husband and live where her father had been born. Soon after arriving there she met a wonderful man and married him soon afterward. It was not long after the marriage took place however, that her husband got terribly ill and died suddenly. Miss Frances chose to remain in England, though alone and grieving.

Not long after her husband died Frances got very ill, as well. When Mr. Everard heard the news he wrote and pleaded with her to return to the colony. He wanted to take care of her along with Dr. McKenzie, who lived just across the Palace Green from their home. Frances did board the next ship back where Mr. Everard waited for her arrival. Once here, her father realized the seriousness of her ill health. He and the good doctor did all they could to help bring her back to health.

Unfortunately, Frances died soon afterward at which time Mr. Everard went mad. That calm, kind man had become so enraged that he has never been able to rid himself of the pain and anger he experienced.

To this day, Mr. Everard can be heard in the late night down in the cellar of the house, screaming out in anger. He blames himself for the death of his daughter, feeling he should have been able to spare her life. He throws things all over the floor of the cellar where workers in the house often have to pick up after him, putting items back on their rightful shelves.

Security guards report seeing Miss Frances and her husband in spirit, out behind the house, in the court yard. They refuse to go behind the house alone.

11. James Geddy House
Duke of Gloucester Street, across Palace Green from Bruton
Parish Church

The James Geddy House was the home and foundry belonging to a family of silversmiths. They crafted bronze, brass, pewter, and silver and also repaired ammunition. Being farther from the capital 'downtown' area of town he had to advertise in the Virginia Gazette to maintain a thriving business.

Today, visitors often hear footsteps above stairs, walking from room to room. Often, workers and guests follow the sounds of a crying baby. After making their rounds through the house they realize it is just the sound of the ghost of a child.

12. Peyton Randolph House
Nicholson and North England Streets

The Peyton Randolph House was built in 1715 for Sir John Randolph, the most distinguished lawyer in Virginia. He was the Clerk of the House of Burgesses and was the only colonial Virginian to be knighted by the King of England. He willed his house to his wife and then his son Peyton, cousin to Thomas Jefferson, who was the son of a Randolph.

Peyton was the Speaker of the House of Burgesses. A very wealthy and influential man Peyton owned several plantations and many slaves, 27 just to run this household. His property in Williamsburg was his small city plantation. He was President of the 1st Continental Congress in 1774 and was elected for a 2nd term. Before fulfilling it he died of an apoplectic stroke or he more than likely would have been the first president of the United States. Peyton's law library combined with George Wythe's are today the nucleus of the Library of Congress.

Peyton's wife Betty continued to live in the house for some years. It was occupied by Count de Rochambeau as a temporary headquarters in 1781 just before the Battle of Yorktown that ended the Revolutionary War. George Washington and Lafayette also dined there after the end of the war.

Peyton and Betty Randolph had prepared a will together before his death. Betty had every intention of following the will once her husband died. Because they had no children they decided to have all their property and slaves auctioned off to just one owner at the time of his death. Before her death, Betty lived alone in the house for some years.

Betty had the reputation of not being terribly kind to her slaves, most especially her personal slave, Eve. Betty blamed Eve for being difficult to get along with, yet the blame belonged to Betty. Upon Peyton's death, Betty seemed to get even more demanding of Eve. She decided to run away. Of course, Mrs. Randolph would not hear of such a thing and made sure someone went out to look for her to bring her back. Unfortunately for Eve, she was found, brought back, and beaten severely. As if that were not enough, Mrs. Randolph changed her will. Everything would still be auctioned off to just one owner except for Eve. She was to be sold to someone several counties away so that she would never be able to see her family again.

The day came after Betty Randolph's death, that Eve was indeed auctioned off and sold. The cart came to the side of the house where she was put face down and chained to the cart. As the horses began pulling the cart from the yard, Eve looked back and screamed for her children, knowing she would never see them again. Then she cursed the house. It became known as a house of sadness and tragedy. Since that time, the house has been filled with mystery, unrest, murders, suicides, illnesses, accidents and much unhappiness.

Many met strange and untimely deaths during the 19th and 20th centuries. There have been at least 2 suicides in the house. One man shot himself in front of the fireplace in the drawing room. Two brothers are known to have gotten into a struggle in the oak paneled bedroom, quite possibly Peyton the Patriot and his brother John, who was a Tory.

Not long after Betty Randolph's death a new family moved into the house. They had a sweet little 6 year old girl. They loved the house and were so pleased that their little girl was so happy, always chattering with an imaginary friend. Then one day the little girl was found at the bottom of the staircase. They thought she had fallen to her death, but upon further medical evaluation, it was realized that the damage that had been done to her body had to have been caused by something of super-human strength. Not long afterward, a man was pushed down the stairs to his death, as well. As a matter of fact, many who work there today have been pushed. If not for holding on to the handrail, they would have fallen to the bottom of the staircase, as well.

The house was sold in 1824 to Mary Peachy who was hostess to Lafayette during his visit to the United States. After the Civil War, a young scholar who had joined the Confederate Army when he was 14, moved into the house while the Peachys lived there. He had lost his family in the war so they took him in. He lived upstairs next to the oak paneled bedroom and attended the College of William and Mary. He developed a severe case of tuberculosis and died a painful and agonizing death, in the house.

Living in the house since their son was 6 years old, the Peachys loved the house. Their little boy especially loved climbing all the trees in the back yard. One day when he was outside climbing trees, it was especially hot. His mother realized that the boy must be thirsty so she took him a drink. When she walked outside she looked for the boy in all the trees. Beginning to get worried, she allowed her eyes to drop to the ground where she found her son lying dead.

From that time on, Mrs. Peachy vowed never to leave the house. She wanted to remain so that she could warn others of the terrible tragedy that takes place there. She has continued with that vow and has never left, even after all these years.

Looking at the front of the house it is easy to spot the two glowing windows above stairs. They happen to be in front of the oak paneled bedroom where Mrs. Peachy resides today. She is often seen as an apparition standing in the corners of that room. As a matter of fact, a Confederate soldier stayed there with his new bride. In the middle of the night they were awaken to the sound of a woman calling their names. When they sat up they saw the spirit of a woman standing there. She appeared to be squeezing her hands, as if to warn them of something unsettling. They also noticed that she was transparent. When she vanished out the window, they ran from the house immediately, never returning for their belongings.

This same scenario has played out over and over, through the years. Owners of the house have refused to sleep in that room, though they store their clothing there. Guests have run from the room, refusing to return.

Mrs. Peachy does not just stay in that bedroom, however. She is often seen and heard in other parts of the house. Those standing outside of the house today often see Mrs. Peachy standing by the front door. At other times she is heard jiggling the front doorknob from the inside of the house. Apparitions are often seen walking inside the house while being watched by guests, from outside. The side door has also been heard slamming a few times in a row, which can be heard across town.

Not long ago a man entered the house through the back door, in the late night. He had the key to let himself in, planning to clean the house, while the house was empty. Soon after he began cleaning he got a feeling that someone was looking in the window at him. He decided to lock himself in so that no one would come in to bother him. He went about cleaning and began hearing whispers behind him. He turned to look and nothing was there. He felt it may be his imagination until he began feeling taps on his shoulders. Again, he looked around and saw nothing, though he was beginning to think it was more than just his imagination. He continued his cleaning, however. Soon afterward, he heard footsteps running up and down the stairs. He went into the front hall to look up the beautiful staircase. He saw nothing, yet the sound of the footsteps continued. At that, he grabbed the house key and ran to the back door. He put the key in the lock as quickly as possible and began turning the key. He turned and he turned and he turned for eight hours and the lock never opened. Of course, he felt like he was going crazy, as the taps felt stronger and the sounds of the whispers and footsteps got much louder as the night progressed. The only reason he got out after eight hours is because another person came to the house to open it up for that day's visitors. When he opened the door the man who had been there all night looked white as a ghost. The man ran from the house and never returned again.

Today, many of the townspeople do not like to even walk by the Peyton Randolph house, even in day light. Some who work for Williamsburg refuse to work in the house.

More recently, there were two security guards who came to the house to check inside to be certain things were in order. As they often did, one stayed outside while the other one took the ring of keys to enter the house. When he went in, he walked around the downstairs where everything seemed to be in order. As he was about to go above stairs he heard the sound of someone talking in the cellar. Believing someone may need his help he went to see what he could do. He opened the cellar door which had not been locked. He walked just two steps down when the cellar door slammed and locked behind him. Though he had planned to go all the way down to see who might be there, he now decided it may be safer not to. Instead, he stood there and listened while trying to get the door to open.

Time went on. What seemed like hours was probably only twenty minutes. As he stood there he was beginning to wonder why the other security guard was not coming in for him. At the same time, the guard outside wondered what happened to the man who went inside. The man on the outside decided to go to the front door that had previously been unlocked. He tried to open the door, but it had locked shut on its own. Not having another set of keys, he decided to knock on the door. When he did, the cellar door mysteriously unlocked and opened and the man was able to get out. However, he was still unable to get out the front door. He later got out the side door. One of Spooks and Legends Haunted Tour's guests professed to the truth of that story. It was his father who was trapped in the cellar that night and he has never returned to the area again, day or night.

While being used as a lodging house, few stayed for the entire night. A man by the name of Mr. Kidman stayed there and was so fearful that he abandoned the house in the middle of the night. He was resting comfortably when he was awakened by a feeling that someone was tugging on his arm. He thought he was dreaming so he rolled over and went back to sleep. A short while later he awoke with a start. He was being shaken violently. As his eyes adjusted to the darkness he could see that he was alone. He ran out of the house as fast as he could and never went back for his belongings.

When the Marquis de Lafayette stayed in the home during his return visit to Williamsburg, he wrote of his ghostly encounter in a letter to his friend. When he arrived at the house he entered through the foyer when he felt a hand on his shoulder. It nudged him as if to keep him from entering. He quickly turned but found no one there. The nights were not restful as the sounds of voices kept him awake for most of his stay.

Throughout the years, many ghostly figures have been seen roaming the empty halls. The old home is filled with dark spirits from all walks of life and many different time periods.

Today, standing in front of the house, taking pictures can prove to be quite an eye-opener. Though one may not think anything is happening while standing there, photos prove otherwise. Often seen in pictures are apparitions, orbs, ghostly faces and skeletal faces as well as hands up against the windows as if trying to summons help.

This is a very haunted and active house, day and night. One woman who once worked in the house recently died. Other workers saw her and spoke with her the next day, not knowing of her death or realizing it was her spirit.

13. Magazine
Duke of Gloucester Street, south side of the street, halfway down

The word 'Magazine' means storage in Arabic. The building was used to store weapons and gun powder. Governor Spotswood designed the Magazine, making it eight sided like a birdhouse. He had also designed the Governor's Palace and Bruton Parish Church. Most of the guns in the building today are original. The powder room is located in the back of the building on the first floor.

During the French and Indian War from 1756-1763 the guardhouse and wall around the magazine were built. Over 60,000 pounds of gunpowder were stored and the residents were afraid of an explosion so they wanted protection. A firefighting machine kept fires from spreading.

On April 21ˢᵗ, 1775 George III told Lord Dunmore to take the powder. When he did, Peyton Randolph made him pay the colonists back. After the Revolution the Magazine was used for many different purposes including a dance studio and a market.

During the Civil War the Magazine was used as a church and then a hospital for wounded soldiers from the south. Northern doctors did their best to help injured soldiers from the north and the south, except for one doctor. He was called the 'Head Devil.' He drank all day and enjoyed brutalizing his patients. Victims suffered mutilation under his care. Amputations were performed needlessly. Piercing screams were heard throughout town as limbs were sawed off. The severed limbs were buried on the property surrounding the building. Over 200 were buried in a mass grave beside the Magazine. They remain there to this day.

Today, people report seeing wounded and crippled soldiers roaming the grounds. Faint sounds can also be heard. Guests of Market Square Tavern, located next to the Magazine, often see a young man in Confederate uniform in the late night hours. He only has one arm which is holding a shovel. Since there are amputation pits on the property, perhaps he is digging to find his missing arm.

Visitors and residents today also report seeing a little girl walking the grounds in the late night. She is dressed in a long white gown and has long flowing hair. Could she be that of a child who once took dance lessons in the converted building?

14. Mary Stith House
Duke of Gloucester Street, south side of the street, capitol end of town

Mary's father, William Stith was the President of the College of William and Mary from 1752 to 1755. Because Mary had never married, her father left everything he owned to her upon his death. She inherited his little house and slaves, whom she treated well. In her will she left everything to them in gratitude for past services. Mary and her slaves are buried together behind the little brick house, which was customary practice of the day.

Backyard Where Bodies are Buried

15. Wetherburn's Tavern
Duke of Gloucester Street, south side of the street on the capitol end of town

One of the most important buildings in town, Wetherburn's Tavern was the most thoroughly documented. There were many different owners of the property over the years, and inventory provided information for restoration.

From 1966 to 1968 extensive archaeological research uncovered nearly 200,000 artifacts on the property. Among them were fifty wine bottles filled with cherries to either preserve them for later, or to use them as brandied cherries.

The tavern offered food, lodging for 7 ½ pence, cards, dice, entertainment and conversation. Balls and meetings were held in the great room which was an addition needed due to the popularity of the tavern. Twelve slaves did everything and lived over the outbuildings. The tavern and dairy are original. The other outbuildings have been reconstructed.

Mr. Wetherburn married Mary Bowcock, widow of the keeper of the Raleigh Tavern. He then inherited her property, gaining the reputation of keeping a good tavern. He later purchased two lots in town across the street from the Raleigh Tavern. There he built Wetherburn's Tavern. He later sold the Raleigh Tavern and he and his family lived at Wetherburn's. When Mary died Henry married Anne Shields, widow of tavern keeper Mr. Shields, who had willed his business and slaves to his widow. Once again, Mr. Wetherburn inherited the business and slaves through his wife. One of its dinner guests was George Washington.

Wetherburn also owned a large farm outside of town. After his death there were several tavern keepers, one being James Southall who renamed the tavern Southall's. Once the capitol moved to Richmond, tavern business declined. The tavern was used as a store, a home, a boarding house and even a girl's school.

One of the employees of Colonial Williamsburg reports that she was alone in the dining room of the tavern one early morning. She had worn her hair in a ponytail that day and had not yet put her cap on. As she walked through the room she suddenly felt like someone was standing behind her, at which time the ribbon was pulled from her hair. Looking back she saw no one, but the ribbon was lying on the floor below.

The spirit of a woman remains in the tavern today. Guests say that she wears a pink gown and has a misty look about her. She stands in the upper left window of the tavern between the blinds and the window pane. The blinds remain perfectly straight behind her as if she is not even there. Suddenly she vanishes before their eyes.

16 .Brickhouse Tavern
Duke of Gloucester Street, south side of the street on the capitol end of town

The Brickhouse Tavern was a nice place for women and children to stay. There was more privacy as there were six doors in the front and six in the back. Unlike the other taverns in town, there were private rooms that did not have to be shared by strangers. Each room had its own separate door for privacy. Women stayed downstairs and men stayed upstairs. It was also frequented by tradesmen who came into town during public times, knowing they could make money giving music lessons or selling their wares right from their private room.

There were two sisters who visited Williamsburg at least once a year. They would stay at the Brickhouse Tavern as they felt very comfortable there. This particular time felt different, however. One night while asleep, one of the women awoke to the smell of pipe smoke and a sweaty body. Upon opening her eyes, she saw the ghost of a man wearing a checkered shirt with the sleeves rolled up to his elbows. He was leaning over her, trying to give her a kiss. She screamed so loudly that her sister awoke and also saw him. This man roams the tavern today, looking for his lost love. When he sees a woman who resembles her he tries to kiss her.

17. Peruke Maker
Duke of Gloucester Street, south side of the street
near the capitol

The wig or peruke maker was very busy. When a man wanted a wig made, a block head was carved in the shape of his head after taking his head measurements. The wig was then made to fit that blockhead perfectly. The work was tedious and the cost of a wig was great.

Wigs were more than a fashion statement. They represented a man's status. Men wore the color wig that coincided with their lot in life. Judges wore white wigs, lawyers wore grey wigs and all others who could afford them wore brown wigs. They were made of goat, yak, horse and human hair. Some of the hair was purchased from Scandinavian girls who were paid in perfume and powder.

There was a man who paid Indians for settlers' scalps. A British officer and former governor-general of Detroit, he was called Henry 'Hair Buyer' Hamilton. He was captured in 1779 and held in a 10x10 foot cell along with six other men. 'In the corner of this snug mansion,' he wrote, 'was fixed a kind of Throne which had ben of use to such miscreants as us for 60 years past and in certain points of wind rendered the air truly Mephytic. Opposite the door ad nearly adjoining the throne was a little Skuttle 5 or 6 inches wide, thro which our Victual was thrust to us.' Hamilton was kept in handcuffs the first night and was fitted in leg irons the next day.

18. King's Arms Tavern
Duke of Gloucester Street, south side of the street
capitol end of town

The King's Arms Tavern is still open today. It serves meals similar to those served in the 18th century. Candlelit rooms and costumed servers give an ambiance to dining that is found nowhere else.

Being at the Capitol end of town it attracted the Burgesses when they were in town on business. Jane Vobe ran the tavern during the Revolution and it was very successful.

Today, guests often meet ghostly visitors while dining there. One visitor went upstairs to the wash room. While standing in front of the mirror, she saw a woman standing behind her in 18th century dress. When she turned around to leave, the woman was gone, though no door had opened and no sound had been made.

It is not a rare occurrence to see a woman walking through the dining room. As she is watched, she suddenly vanishes through the wall.

A woman by the name of Irma was the inn keeper at one time, and lived in the upstairs of the tavern. One day she did not come down as she always had before. One of the workers went up to see where she was. When he got to her bedroom door he opened it, as she had not answered when he called her name. There on the bedroom floor was Irma's dead body. Her spirit has never left the tavern since that day. The light in that room is often seen going on and off in the late night.

Irma enjoys entertaining guests still today. She is known to throw menus from stands and blow candles out. After the tavern has been prepared for the following day, the workers go home. Upon their arrival the next day, chairs have been pulled out from tables. It is believed that Irma still wants to welcome guests as she did when she was the innkeeper.

Right out front of the tavern is a pole with a bucket of tar and sack of feathers hanging from it. This is where a person would be tarred and feathered for all to see, if they dared to speak against the king. After the Revolution, the tavern's name changed to the Eagle Tavern.

19. Shields Tavern
Duke of Gloucester Street, south side of street
near the Capitol

Though Shield's Tavern is close to the Capitol, it surprisingly attracted lower gentry and successful middling customers. Craftsmen, farmers and artisans frequented the tavern. It is one of four taverns in town that continues to be open to dining guests, still today.

Mr. Marot owned this tavern and was murdered inside, by a close friend. He is still seen walking up to guests' tables, glances at their food and then walks away and vanishes.

Mr. Marot is known to hold door handles tightly, making it nearly impossible for a guest to open the doors upstairs. The door knob rattles though there is no hand on it. He enjoys teasing guests and making his presence known.

20. Palmer House
Duke of Gloucester Street, south side of street, last house before the Capitol

The Civil War took place from 1861-1865. In 1862 Gen. Johnston, Gen. McClellan and Col. Campbell appreciated the town and instructed their troops not to be destructive. The Confederates captured Campbell and put him in a prison in Richmond. The Union troops retaliated and burned the Wren Building at the College of William and Mary, but the Palmer House was spared. Looking at the house today, you can see what are called 'put log' holes in the bricks. They were used for scaffolding while working on the house. Today, apples are put in those holes at Christmas time for decoration.

Because the Palmer House was home to many soldiers during the Civil War, one such soldier is still seen in the house today. One woman who lived there reported a 'ghostly presence' lurking in her home. She would go downstairs in the late night to get a glass of water. That is when she would come in contact with this man. She said he was a transparent figure sitting in a chair smoking a pipe. He was dressed in 'dark clothing with gold trim' she said, sitting cross legged reading a book. She fell to the floor from fear. It is believed to be Mr. Disosway, a federal lieutenant who died in the house. She later got used to the man and claimed he was kind with a friendly smile. He is now a permanent resident of the house.

21. Capitol
East end of Duke of Gloucester Street

The Capitol is a very beautiful building. It is shaped in the form of an 'H.' There are two sides, one for the king and one for the people. The Upper House was comprised of the governor and twelve members of the general court, appointed by the king. The Lower House was comprised of the Burgesses. In order to be considered to be a Burgess, one had to be at least 21 years of age, white, male, a landowner (at least 50 acres outside of Williamsburg), Anglican and elected by the people. Just two men were considered from each county. There were 140 members by the time of the Revolution plus one from the College of William and Mary, one from Williamsburg, one from Norfolk and one from Jamestown.

The room over the piazza which joined both sides of the Capitol, was a joint conference room. The Council was the Upper House and the Burgesses was the Lower House. The third floor was where the jury met. There was no light, no heat, no food or water available. The door was locked to ensure a quick decision before dark. Capitol crimes were horse stealing, forgery, arson, murder and more.

The Great Union flag (a large 'X' with no stripes) became the national standard of Great Britain and her colonies in 1606. It flies over the Capitol today. The Grand Union flag (a small 'x' with stripes) became the first American flag to fly in Williamsburg on May 15th, 1776.

It is a misconception that Patrick Henry gave his 'Give Me Liberty' speech at the Capitol in Williamsburg. He gave his 'Caesar Brutus' speech there, but his 'Give Me Liberty' speech was given at St. John's Church in Richmond in 1776.

This is the town where Grace Sherwood was tried for being a witch. Some say she remains in the Capitol in the darkest of night. Often when a reenactment of her trial is underway today, Grace's spirit is seen in the gallery looking out over the courtroom.

Blackbeard the pirate stole treasure from any vessel that dared to get in his way. He was friends with the governor of North Carolina and shared his bounty with him. Consequently, Governor Spotswood had to send ships to Blackbeard's hideout off Ocracoke Island in North Carolina. Blackbeard boarded Robert Maynard's sloop. Pistols shot and cutlasses clashed in combat.

Blackbeard was shot and cut many times, but kept fighting until he finally fell dead on the sloop. The other pirates surrendered. Maynard had Blackbeard's head severed and then hung it from the ship. When his body was thrown overboard into the cold water, it is said that Blackbeard swam around the ship several times before he sank.

When Maynard returned to Virginia, Blackbeard's head was mounted on a high pole at the mouth of the Hampton River. For many years it was a warning to others. The site is still known as Blackbeard's Point.

The skull was later taken down and made into a large punch bowl which was used as a drinking vessel at the Raleigh Tavern.

The remaining fifteen or sixteen pirates stood trial in Williamsburg. All were convicted except one and were sentenced to be hanged. Samuel Odell was the only man acquitted. He had been on the ship only one day and had not participated in any villainous acts at sea. Later, Israel Hands was also pardoned. He died a beggar on the streets of London.

22. Secretary's Office and Jones Graveyard
East end of Duke of Gloucester Street next to the
Capitol

When the Capitol building burned in 1747 many public records were destroyed. In 1748, the Public Records Office or Secretary's Office was built. To deter fire, no attic or basement was added to the building. The interior walls were made of plaster laid on brick, and the floor was made of stone. Very little wood was used, though there are several fireplaces. Heat was needed to keep the papers from getting moldy.

Near the turn of the century the Secretary's Office became the home of David Roland Jones and his family of seven girls. He had his family buried less than twenty feet away from the home, which is where the small graveyard remains today.

Mr. Jones was very strict with his daughters. He would not allow them to leave the house, which is why they were often seen sitting on the front lawn playing with their cats.

His daughter, Edna was getting older and often spoke with John, the delivery boy. They were planning to meet by the Palace one night. After her family went to bed, Edna got all dressed up and waited until everyone was asleep. When she finally left the house, she ran as fast as she could toward the Palace. She had terrible eyesight and wore very thick glasses. While she was running, she did not see the carriage coming toward her. As it was coming at quite a speed, the carriage hit her and left her in the road to die. So afraid of her father's punishment for leaving the house, her spirit returned home as quickly as possible.

Edna is still in fear of her father. Guests standing near the graveyard can often see her hovering over the graves in the late night. They hear lonely Edna calling out while they pass by.

23. Public Gaol (Jail)
East end of Nicholson Street, north side of street

The jail was built in 1704. Two original cells remain. If sentenced to die the criminal had ten days to get his affairs in order. The upstairs of the house was where the insane and women debtors were kept. On average there were 2 hangings per year. Since Williamsburg was the Capitol of Virginia during most of the 18th century, any free person accused of a felony had to be tried in the city. During this period, there was little compromise in the judicial process. If a person was convicted of murder, arson, horse stealing, forgery or piracy, he or she was often sentenced to hang. As a result, Williamsburg was the scene of numerous hangings.

It was thought to be inhumane and cruel to keep a criminal confined in a cell for a prolonged period of time. Hanging was considered a kinder punishment than imprisonment. Cells were small, cramped and unheated. Windows had no glass to protect prisoners from the elements. They slept on piles of insect-ridden straw. Heavy shackles were used to chain prisoners to the floor. Lice covered the walls and roaches and rodents scurried throughout the cells. The smell was almost unbearable.

Debtors, insane military prisoners, British Redcoats, Tory sympathizers, spies, mentally ill women and runaway slaves were held in prison. Around noon on the day of the execution, the condemned was taken from the gaol. Placed on a cart, sitting on his own coffin, he was attended by a clergyman. When the criminal arrived at the gallows he was the center of a social event. Public hangings brought people to the Capitol from all over the surrounding countryside. It was usually a festive cheering crowd that greeted the prisoner when he or she arrived. The sheriff, also the hangman, was waiting at the gallows as well.

The cart was pulled beneath the gallows where the criminal was allowed to speak his last words. The noose was then placed around his neck after which time he was 'turned off the cart' as the horses pulled away. He was left to hang until death. Not all men died easily so he was often relieved to see a friend out in the crowd who would be kind enough to go over and pull on his legs to quickly break his neck. After the hangings, the bodies were often strung up for public viewing as a warning to others.

One of the more noted trials in Williamsburg was of several members of Blackbeard's crew guilty of heinous crimes. They were hanged just outside of town, at the gallows.

In the Spring of 1719, the remaining pirates were taken by ox-drawn carts from the gaol to the gallows. They were transported to what is now called Capitol Landing Road, then called Gallows Road. Townspeople gathered with picnic baskets to watch the hangings.

A man by the name of Peter Pelham was the jail keeper. He and his family lived at the jail in a couple of enclosed rooms on the first floor. The kitchen was below the house and up above was where the insane and women debtors stayed. There were 4 cells in the back and hangings averaged two per year. Gaol keepers were poorly paid which is why Peter Pelham also worked as the organist of the Bruton Parish church. He took the prisoners who were condemned to death to church the Sunday before their hanging took place. This gave the convict a chance to make things right with God. They were also given the job of pumping the organ for Mr. Pelham as he played.

Haunting stories of the Wagon of Death have been reported ever since. People living on Nicholson Street hear the sounds of a horse and wagon in the early morning hours. They dash to their windows but see nothing.

One visitor at the Coke-Garrett house, which is next to the jail, was sleeping in a room facing Nicholson Street. He woke to the sound of horses and the cracking of a whip. A loud gruff voice commanded the animals to move faster. The visitor ran to the window remembering about the Wagon of Death. He saw nothing.

Many who visit today and who stay over on Hangman's Road hear the wagon, the horses and the cheering crowds in the early morning hours. The sounds then vanish away.

24. Pasteur & Galt Apothecary
Duke of Gloucester Street, north side of the street, east end

Both doctors Pasteur and Galt were apothecary surgeons. They later studied at St. Thomas's Hospital in London. They practiced in partnership from 1775-1778. The shop now displays copies of Dr. Galt's certificates in surgery, anatomy, midwifery and general medicine. Today the shop has antique English and Dutch jars, pharmaceutical equipment, a traveling medical kit, surgical tools, leeches and a human skeleton which hangs in the examination room.

During the 18th century, this is where you would go to have your teeth pulled. A tooth key was used, which gripped the tooth and then twisted it out of the socket. Surgeries and amputations were also performed.

Tooth Key

25. Raleigh Tavern
Duke of Gloucester Street, north side of the street,
east end

The Raleigh Tavern was established in 1717. It was named for Sir Walter Raleigh who had attempted the first colonization of Virginia in 1585. During Publick Times in April and October, planters and merchants from all over the colony passed beneath Sir Walter Raleigh's bust, which remains over the door today. The Tavern gained some fame in the pre-Revolution as a gathering place for the elected legislative body. Several Royal Governors officially dissolved the House of Burgesses when their actions did not suit the Crown. They then met in the Tavern. Such dissension became more common between the end of the French and Indian War in 1763 and the outbreak of the American Revolution in 1776.

In 1769, the Burgesses were dissolved by Governor Botetourt for disrespect, for protesting the Townsend Acts. Thomas Jefferson, Patrick Henry, George Washington and others reconvened in the Apollo Room. They adopted the Non-Importation Agreement to suspend the purchase of various goods from British merchants.

The Burgesses planned the Revolutionary War and the siege of Yorktown. It might have been called a boycott, but the word would not be invented for another 111 years. On May 27th, Gov. Dunmore dissolved the House of Burgesses again, for objecting to the closing of the Port of Boston after its Tea Party. Eighty-nine Burgesses reassembled at the Raleigh Tavern to form another non-importation association. George Mason drafted the association agreement and George Washington introduced it.

Phi Beta Kappa was founded here in 1776 and the Raleigh Tavern was considered an institution at that time. It is where balls and auctions were held, as well. George Washington dined in the tavern and was given a birthday party in the Apollo Room. Patrick Henry was also honoured there in a farewell dinner. Theater tickets were sold at the Raleigh Tavern and merchandise and slaves were auctioned from its steps. Many leading Virginians dined here and it is also where the Marquis de Lafayette was entertained at a banquet in 1824.

The building remained in continuous use as a tavern until it burned at the hands of an arsonist in 1859. The Raleigh Tavern, an L-shaped white weatherboard building with 18 dormer windows, was rebuilt between 1929 and 1932 on original foundations. It stands as a testament that the work of a democracy does not require a fancy building to function, quite a contrast to the Capitol Building. Painted in gilt above the mantle in Apollo Room it says, *Hilaritas sapientiae et bonae vitae proles* (jollity is the offspring of wisdom and good living).

Behind the tavern stands the 18th century kitchen where today's visitors can purchase cookies, bread, soda, coffee and other baked goods.

While guests today stand in front of the Tavern one can smell delicious sweet potato muffins. There was once a woman who baked those delicious muffins and sold them out in the street. Her spirit and the aroma of her goods are still a part of this town.

Even after all this time, some hear the sounds of a party going on inside the Raleigh Tavern. Spirits dance in the Apollo Room, as if they were still attending the many balls that took place in the 18th century. The smell of pipe smoke is still very strong. When one goes over to look in the windows however, there is only darkness.

26. James Craig Silversmith
Sign of the Golden Ball
Duke of Gloucester Street, north side of the street
east end

James Craig was an excellent jeweler and silversmith. A good part of his success was due to the fact that his shop was downtown near the Capitol. That end of town was always busiest since the Burgesses stayed in that area when court met four times a year.

Mr. Craig was from London. He lived within his shop with his family of five and one slave.

In the 18th century slaves were held in chains in the basement, until the time came for them to be auctioned off and sold. Today their spirits are heard rattling chains in the late night. Benches shake and sounds of chatter can be heard in the dead of night.

27. Prentis Store
Duke of Gloucester Street, north side of the street halfway down

Prentis Store is one of Williamsburg's best surviving examples of a colonial store. It is a 1740 original structure which was a highly successful general store until the time of the Revolution. Its architecture is typical of a store of that day. The door above the front door in the gable area was used to lift merchandise into the loft.

In the 20th century before restoration took place, the building was used as a gas station. Fortunately it was not altered much at all. It was very much in its original state at the time of restoration.

Mr. Prentis was known to be an angry man who did not like women. He would lock his wife away on the upper floor of the store. He still seems to be angry. His spirit throws things at women who are working in the store today. His wife's spirit can be seen floating from room to room and items fly off of shelves. Mr. Prentis later had his wife committed to the hospital for insane and disordered minds, just one road over. Many believe he drove her mad.

28. Tayloe House
Nicholson Street, north side of street

Col. John Tayloe was one of the wealthiest men in Virginia and was a justice of the peace. He owned a plantation called Mr. Airy in Richmond County. He stayed in this house whenever he came to Williamsburg.

During the Revolution, Williamsburg became a place where fighting soldiers could get equipment repaired and horses shod. Townspeople supplied the Patriot soldiers with blankets, clothing, food and lodging. Military troops built a large encampment behind the Tayloe House. The Patriot forces found the back wooded property an excellent site for encampment. The colonel did not support the struggle for freedom, however. Though he was a close friend of George Washington, he could not support the cause. Hundreds of soldiers continued to camp on the wooded lot behind his home. Some injured in Yorktown were brought back to the grounds to be treated. After the war ended the grounds were vacant.

The little building next door was Mr. Tayloe's office. It has a very interesting 'ogee' shaped roof. One woman who recently lived there had a cat. The cat had a ball he often played with. Many nights the ball would roll on its own. The woman said it looked like someone was playing with the cat, perhaps a young child. The cat would bat at the ball with his paw, which kept the woman and the cat amused most evenings.

This same lady later lived in the Tayloe house next door. While living there she reported hearing troops out in back of her house late in the night. She would go look out the back windows to find soldiers sitting around campfires as she smelled the fire and heard the soldiers' laughter. As soon as the sound of the troops stopped, so did the sight of the soldiers. Horses and carriages could be heard going right past the house at night. When she would look outside she saw nothing. Often 18th century music could be heard. Being so close to the Palace, it is possible that it was music coming from the many parties which took place at the Governor's home.

Guests in town as well as residents often report the same sight out behind that very house. When guests walk to the back yard to observe however, the sounds and sights have vanished and everything is black.

Tayloe Office

29. Ludwell Paradise House
Duke of Gloucester Street, north side of street, about halfway
down

The first house to be purchased by John D. Rockefeller, Jr.
in 1926 for $8,000

Philip Ludwell III lived in the Ludwell-Paradise House in
1755. He rented it as a tenement for many years. William and
Clementina Rind lived there and also printed the Virginia Gazette
in the house. Mr. Ludwell's daughter, Lucy Ludwell married John
Paradise, a scholar. She lived in the house in the 1800s. Lucy was
eccentric at best. Had she not been from a well to do family she
probably would have been committed to a mental institution, at a
very young age.

Her husband John took Lucy back to London where they
lived together during the Revolution. It got back to the colony that
she had taken boiling hot water from her tea urn and thrown it on
a man who annoyed her.

Lucy's grandfather had built this house which she inherited. The house was confiscated during the Revolution because her husband was a Tory. In 1805, ten years after her husband died, Lucy came back to America and was allowed to have her house back. Everyone talked about how odd she was. Because of her social position in London, she considered herself above her friends and neighbors in Virginia. She preferred that people call her Madame.

When the future President, James Monroe came to Williamsburg, she ran up to him and said 'Sir, we have determined to make you president.' She also borrowed new clothes from her lady friends. Before returning the gowns she would cut holes in them and render them useless. She thought she was a fashion plate of her time and was oblivious to the fact that everyone in town knew she was wearing borrowed clothes. On Sunday mornings Lucy regularly had 'her little black boy,' her servant's son, carry her prayer book into church ahead of her, as if to announce her entrance.

She entertained guests on weird carriage rides. She had a favorite coach reassembled on the back porch and would invite guests for a ride. Her servant would roll it back and forth on the porch taking her guests on imaginary trips. These carriage rides became frequent as she was having a hard time differentiating between reality and make-believe. Consequently, in 1812 she was committed to the state asylum across town.

Lucy's spirit remains in the house today. She is often seen looking out one of the upstairs windows in the late night. Residents who now live in the house report hearing her bathing several times a day. She had done the same before her death, as she had a bath fetish.

30. Coke-Garrett House
East end of Nicholson Street next to the Gaol

The Coke-Garrett House is of Greek Revival architecture. The west portion also has Chinese Chippendale railing. The home was used as a tavern at one time in its history. Two of its residents, Mr. Coke was a silversmith and Mr. Garrett, a doctor.

Being right next to the gaol, there are many stories that go with the house pertaining to the hangings that took place. Because Nicholson Street is where the carts rode on their way to the gallows, those who have stayed in the house report hearing the Wagon of Death riding down the road. Horses are heard making snort and whinny sounds as whips crack in the night. When residents or guests look out their window to see the cart, there is nothing there.

Later in its history, Dr. Garrett used the small building next to the house as his apothecary or doctor's office. During the Civil War, many of the soldiers staggered to his office, writhing in pain, from the fields of the Battle of Williamsburg. He was very kind to the soldiers from both sides and the men all knew he would treat them well and fairly. He was known as the doctor who would take care of half severed arms and legs.

So many amputations were needed that the doctor did not have time to bury the severed limbs. Consequently, they were piling up reaching as high as the window sill. The office became so full of blood that people slipped and fell to the floor. Blood ran down the streets.

The dead were wrapped in sheets and buried in mass graves. Amputation pits were eventually dug to bury the dozens of limbs accumulating every day.

Civil War soldiers are still seen wandering the property in the late night. One young Confederate soldier is seen lying on the grounds, heard writhing in pain.

Dr. Garrett's Apothecary

81

31. Courthouse / Pillory and Stock
Duke of Gloucester Street, halfway down

The Courthouse was built in 1770 and was used for more than 150 years. The Hustings court (city of Williamsburg) met on the 1st Monday of the month and the James City County Court met on the 2nd Monday of the month. Each lasted several days. County court crimes included absence from church, gossip, wife-beating, drunkenness and pig or chicken stealing. Punishments were public flogging at the whipping post and / or being locked in the stocks or pillory. All blacks were tried in the county court. General court met in April and October and the Court of Oyer and Terminer (hear and decide) met in December and June.

Being left in the pillory or stock for a long day was not pleasant. In the stock, one sat on a very hard rail with his ankles locked between two planks of wood in front of him. The pillory was not very comfortable either, as one would stand bent forward with his neck and wrists between holes in two planks of wood. Townspeople and those from out of town would throw rotted food at the condemned. They would be teased relentlessly for a full day. In the pillory, because it was expected for the head to stay straight up, the person's ears were nailed to the wood. At the end of the day the nails were not removed from the person's ears, the ears were removed from the nails. One would be said to be 'ear marked' for life.

Today, visitors can put themselves into the pillory and stock and have their picture taken by a friend or family member.

Pillory and Stock

32. Matthew Whaley School
Scotland Street

* I would be remiss if I were not to include the wonderful and heartwarming story of little Matthew Whaley. I do hope you all enjoy this story as much as I do...... Bonnie*

When the Capitol moved to Williamsburg in 1699, there were families who already lived in town. One such family was the Whaleys. Mr. James Whaley was instrumental in helping Francis Nicholson design the new city and worked hard on its plans.

Not long afterward, Mr. Whaley died, leaving his wife Mary Paige behind as well as his son Matthew. Fortunately, James was of gentry class so there was no shortage of wealth with which to raise Matthew. The responsibility that Mary Paige carried, however, was much to bear alone. Matthew, being of gentry class, had to be readied to begin his education at the College of William and Mary.

At the time of James' death, Matthew was 5 years old so he needed to begin serious studies to be readied for college by the young age of thirteen. Mary Paige had been a teacher so she had the knowledge, though she would be taking this on alone, along with caring for the household and many slaves.

Mary Paige was very dedicated to Matthew so she took it all in stride and began teaching him at home. Matty was doing so well in his studies, but did not easily make friends. Mary Paige was concerned especially since he had just suffered the loss of his father. He needed friends to keep his mind off his father's death.

Mrs. Whaley could not accept such sadness in the little boy, so she welcomed other gentry children into her home to be educated along with Matty. She was so hopeful for some friendships to develop between the children, yet Matthew still was not making friends.

After some time, Matty came home with a friend he had met in town. His name was Toby. He was such a nice little boy, a slave's son from just down the road. Mrs. Whaley loved Toby and was so happy that he and Matthew seemed to enjoy each other's company so much. They played together as often as they could.

Mrs. Whaley knew that the friendship would come to an end should town gentry find out that they were friends. Gentry children were not to play with slave children, most especially if from different households. Kindly, Mrs. Whaley decided to teach Toby at a different time of day so that he also could get an education.

A wonderful woman, she was so happy that the boys not only continued to be good friends, but that their friendship grew more every day.

By the time the boys were nine years old they were inseparable. Sadly, one of the boys contracted tuberculosis. Soon afterward, the other one contracted it as well. Neither life was saved. Mrs. Whaley was heartbroken. She loved both boys so much and was lost without them.

Matty was buried on top of his father's grave in the Bruton Parish Cemetary. Toby, by law, was to be buried behind his master's house on some non-descript piece of land. Mrs. Whaley, however, could not bear for the boys to be separated in death. She secretly had Toby's body buried with Matty's and Mr. Whaley's, in the church yard.

So distraught, Mary Paige decided she would return to England. Before leaving however, she wanted to have a school built in memory of her son. She left funds behind to make that dream a reality.

The first Matthew Whaley School was built on the east end of town and was quickly outgrown. When the second school needed to be built, it was placed on Palace Green. That school was later taken down when the Governor's Palace, which had burned years earlier, was to be reconstructed. The third school is still in use today and is on the west end of town, just two blocks north of Duke of Gloucester Street.

Today, many report seeing Matthew and Toby playing on the field, out behind the school. Janitors hear strange things at night from within its walls. Running footsteps are heard in the hallways and also on the third floor. Many past students speak of strange things happening in the school when they attended. They would see the boys and then they would vanish before their eyes.

It was a wonderful gift that Mrs. Whaley left to this town. What is most important in the story, however, is not that she left a school named after her son, Matthew Whaley, but the way in which she left it. Funds were given with the stipulation that the school had to educate children from all walks of life and all classes of society. Without that promise kept, all funds were to be returned to her.

Personally, I am so very proud of Mrs. Whaley and the way she lived her life. She lived according to what her heart told her to do, though she could very well have been ridiculed by others and even reprimanded. Because of her goodness, she has touched many lives over the years, including those who still attend the school, named in memory of her little boy.

Perhaps you will not remember one thing about this book. I am not concerned with that. I do hope, however, that you remember Mary Paige Whaley for the way she lived her life. If you live your life, following your heart, not worrying about what others think, you too will forever be at peace.......forever at peace.

In 1705, Matthew's mother buried him beneath a stone that says:

"Matthew Whaley lies Interred here
Within this Tomb upon his father dear
Who Departed
this life the 26th
of September 1705 Aged
Nine years only child
of James Whaley
and Mary his wife."

"Matthew Whaley lies Interred here
Within this Tomb upon his father dear
Who Departed
this life the 26th
of September 1705 Aged
Nine years only child
of James Whaley
and Mary his wife."

Inscription on Matthew Whaley's Tomb

Statue of Matthew in Front of the School

33. Meet the Ghost of Catherine Rathell
Played by Bonnie Florek in Tours and Performance
Monologues

Catherine Rathell returns today as she tells haunting stories of her past life in Williamsburg. She came to Virginia from Liverpool, England in 1765.

As a milliner and mantua maker (similar to a 21st century dressmaker), she owned her own shop on Capitol Square, in the Ascough House. She was very successful as her shop was so very close to where the Burgesses met at the Capitol. Even the wives of the Burgesses came into town and utilized Catherine's fine dressmaking skills.

The ghostly character of Catherine Rathell likes to tell of the time Mr. Henry came into her shop to purchase artificial calves to place inside his stockings. He was most demanding of her, insisting she open her shop before the sun had even risen that day. She was not surprised it was that 'dreadful man' demanding her attention. She was not happy with Mr. Henry or Mr. Jefferson. After all, shopkeepers were at a great loss once importation from England was no longer allowed. How were these shop owners going to support themselves and their families, without the fine British goods and supplies they needed to successfully continue in business?

Since Catherine Rathell was a widow with no one to help support her, she was at a great loss without importation of the finest of British fabrics and goods, not available here in the colonies. She had to make the difficult decision to go back to England 'till Liberty of Importation is Allowed.' Unfortunately, on her voyage back to her homeland, ship 'Peggy' sank in sight of Liverpool. Her body may lie in the bottom of the ocean today, where it is cold, but her spirit remains in the Capitol City of Williamsburg, the town she always intended to return to.

The ghost of Catherine leads visiting guests of Spooks and Legends Haunted Tours through town. She also offers monologues based on Catherine and other 18th century townspeople. She tells of the many haunts and ghosts in town. Catherine is a very nice ghost though she tells of the other types of ghosts here, as well.

34. Meet the Ghost of Lucy Ludwell

Lucy Ludwell comes alive straight from the Public Hospital for Insane and Disordered Minds. She was considered a 'lunitick' during the time of the Revolution, and her ghost proves that name suits her perfectly.

Coming back to the colony from England, after her husband had died, proved to be quite a shock to her and her friends. Upon returning, she asked Thomas Jefferson to return her home to her, a home that had been taken over after she left during the Revolution. He granted her wish. She was left with nothing except the house.

Lucy tells of her own crazy antics. She questions why the townspeople think she needs to be committed. Having ladies over for tea proved to be quite interesting. Since she did not have horses any longer, her carriage sat on her back porch. After tea she would invite her lady friends to go for carriage rides. She had her one remaining slave push the carriage back and forth, as she commented on what a beautiful ride it was, pointing things out 'along the way.'

She thought nothing of pouring hot tea on a man's lap while in England, just because she was annoyed by him. Lucy explains that her motive was justified, as she did not like the man.

Lucy Ludwell now enjoys taking guests of Spooks and Legends Haunted Tours through a different part of town from Catherine. She shares stories of her ghostly friends of Williamsburg. Her eccentricity makes for an interesting walk through town or a fun monologue performance.

ABOUT THE AUTHOR

Bonnie has been a business owner for many years. As a dressmaker and graduate of Maison Sapho School of Dressmaking in New York City, she was the owner of a home-based business while raising her children. Bonnie has also earned a degree in social work.

Raised a United Methodist minister's daughter, Bonnie is often called a 'PK,' short for 'Preacher's Kid.' A church organist in the past, she also directed adult and children's choirs, brass ensembles and hand bell choirs. She is an extensively trained soprano and has performed a solo concert at the Crystal Cathedral in California, home church of the Rev. Robert Schuller. In addition, Bonnie is a Christian recording artist, an accomplished cellist and flutist, and has taught many children to play the piano.

For several years Bonnie has written for many publications, most recently the Examiner. As a certified Reiki Master she also maintains a professional practice in town, Reiki Health and Healing .

In addition, Bonnie is the owner and creator of the most haunted tour in Williamsburg, Virginia, USA. Having personally experienced many ghosts, she has created a one-of-a-kind tour based on fully researched ghost stories. She also performs monologues for various groups in the area.

Bonnie resides in Williamsburg, Virginia with husband Tom Florek, daughter Julie Eynard, son Eric Redmond II, and grandchildren Jaycee Redmond and Eric Redmond III.

ABOUT SPOOKS AND LEGENDS
HAUNTED TOURS, LLC

From start to finish, a Spooks and Legends Haunted Tour is engaging, fun for all ages and most importantly, based on fully researched ghost stories and reported sightings. Being so unique, it has become the #1 tour choice in Williamsburg in just a few short years. Williamsburg is a very haunted town yet most tours do not fully embrace that truth.

Spooks and Legends tours are led by an 18th century costumed 'ghost guide' who becomes the character of a real person who lived in town during the Revolution. As guests become engaged they forget that the guide is a real living person. It is a very realistic tour with other town characters often meeting the tour group along the way, as they walk the eerie streets of the old haunted town.

Guests have attended from all over the world including the Netherlands, England, India, Canada, France, Russia, and Germany. Spooks and Legends' excellent Trip Advisor reviews say it all.

New to our tours this year are child characters 'Elizabeth and James Geddy,' played by Jaycee Redmond and Eric Redmond, III. This is especially exciting for our younger guests. These 18th century children give the tour a personal touch for all ages.

For more information or to attend an ever-popular Spooks and Legends Tour, please go to our website: www.spooksandlegends.com or contact Bonnie directly at: spooksandlegends@aol.com / 1-757-784-6213. Bonnie is also available for monologue performances. We look forward to meeting you and giving you an experience of a lifetime.

** If you would like to have your venue featured in one of Bonnie's up-coming books, please submit information regarding your ghost tour, haunted walk, or other ghostly location. Any and all information will be considered for one of her two new book series *Totally Haunted USA* or *Totally Haunted UK*. Please contact her by email or phone. She will choose the most interesting, most haunted submissions to include in her upcoming books. Those who contribute will get special recognition for their venue.

www.spooksandlegends.com
spooksandlegends@aol.com

757-784-6213

Don't forget to LIKE us on Facebook
Please review this book on Amazon.com and Amazon.uk. Should you write a book, I will be happy to read it and write a review for you as well. Thank you so much. *BOO!*

THANK YOU TO FRED VICK

I would like to personally thank Fred Vick for his excellent character interpretation. Without his talents, our tours would not be the success that they are. He is a real asset to Spooks and Legends Haunted Tours, playing several different ghost characters. As 'Peter Pelham,' the town jailer and church organist, his interactions with 'Catherine Rathell' prove to be quite interesting. He stops to greet guests on his way to yet another town tavern, while also searching for some of his escaped convicts.

A big thank you to Fred!

NEW TOUR CHARACTERS

Eric Redmond III and Jaycee Redmond
'James and Elizabeth Geddy'

TOUR SIGHTINGS

Church Graveyard

Peyton Randolph House

Grissell Hay House

Nelson Galt House

Ludwell Paradise House

George Wythe House

TRIP ADVISOR TOUR REVIEWS

"Loved it!"

Interesting, informative, fun! Tour guide was greatly entertaining.   Can't wait to take her other tour!

Visited April 2014
Medora, IN

"Very well done."

The hostess knows her stuff and articulated it very well. Didn't see any ghosts but thoroughly enjoyed the stories and the walk. Just the right length, 1 1/4 hrs, We were lucky enough to have a beautifully pleasant evening for the tour,(4/11) with a creepy ring around the big moon. Thanks Spooks and Legends!

Visited April 2014
Robin D

"Very Creative Tour"

I wasn't really sure what to expect when I signed my family up for this tour so when we started out and she informed us that it wasn't going to be a history lesson I was very surprised. I really liked all of the stories that we heard and the perspective in which she told them. We will definitely be coming back for another tour.

Visited March 2014
Liverpool, NY

"Enjoyable night"

Even in the chilly air it was a very enjoyable tour around the old town. Our guide had great legends and stories of the town folk from the early years. Great hour of entertainment at a very reasonable price. Kinda wish the stragglers of the group could keep up but can't do much about that. She was nice enough to wait for them at each stop. Wondering what the new tour will have to offer

Visited February 2014
Rehoboth, DE

"Great time"

Fun and entertaining! The stories are very interesting and make you want to see more. Will go again.

Visited May 2014
Richmond, VA

"A must do!"

In full costume and character, Catherine and Fred will give you the best ghost tour in Williamsburg VA. A great time at a great value. Thank you so much, we had a wonderful evening. To those of you who are parents, if you feel you HAVE to bring children on this tour, please only bring along mature quiet children. Adults are trying to have fun. Thank you.

Visited April 2014
CoupleInTheir40s

"Great Time Despite Rain"

We had a group of 30 teenagers in Williamsburg for a choral competition so we decided to do the tour after the competition and dinner. Our dinner ran later than expected and Spooks and Legends graciously worked with us to move the tour to half an hour later. Our hostess had their attention from the beginning and they didn't even complain about the rain. Loved that our guide was in character during the tour. Very enjoyable experience.

Visited April 2014
Joann C

"Entertaining!"

Very informative! Wonderful opportunity to learn the history of the "other" side of WIlliamsburg. We got lots of great "sketches". We will definitely be taking the new tour.

Visited April 2014
Dana J

"Great time!"

Cold night, perfect for sending the chills right down your spine!! Good time and very informative, loved it!!!

Visited January 2014
Summerville,SC

"spooks and legends ghost walk"

Highly recommend this event, Bonnie our host was fabulous, she was wonderful and loved her approach to the stories she told, we got some great pics of orbs in the area. will def do this again our next time in the area. Thanks so much bonnie for all you put into your ghost walk. enjoyed it all from start to finish. Again, Fabulous..................

Visited December 2013
Newark, DE

"Fun for entire family!"

Our entire family went (2-62), and we all had a great time! We bundled up for the Christmas tour, and it was very well done. Even our kids (almost 9, 7 and 4) were into the story and didn't mind the cold hour and a half long walk. Wish we had been told to bring our real camera though as cell phone cameras just can't capture what you want at night. Other than that it was very entertaining, and we enjoyed ourselves very much! Use restroom before you go. Would highly recommend.

Visited December 2013
Williamsburg, VA

"Well done"

Very well conducted. Rainy early evening did not make a negative impact. The booking was simple to do – voicemail got responded to. Even the children enjoyed the hour long walk.

Visited November 2013
Kolkata

"Wonderful Night!"

I booked Spooks & Legends for a social event for an organization at the College and I would do it again in a heartbeat!
Bonnie and Mr. Vick were both delightful and thoroughly entertaining. I cannot speak enough for their professionalism, showmanship, knowledge and warmth. We were a group of about 40 graduate students, and each person reported the same great experience.
Highly recommended!

Visited October 2013
Williamsburg, VA

"Great tour & great experience! Would go again if we lived closer."

Bonnie was wonderful. I was very happy that I decided on this haunted tour for my husband and I to go on. It was our last night in Williamsburg that we took the tour at end of September. I think it was a great way to end our vacation.

I am going to start off by saying that this is not a haunted house, people jumping out at you kinda tour. I think a lot of people, especially the young crowd think that. On our tour some younger girl made a comment "this isn't scary". Yes because it's a walking tour and you hear the true tails of Williamsburg. You may see or hear things and capture orbs and such in your photos like I was able and from what I saw on other photos many other people did to. My husband is not one for this type of stuff but, I am and he was happy to go. We both enjoyed it. I received an email from Bonnie after the tour. She was hoping we enjoyed our tour and would love to hear feedback, positive or negative. I had all positive. I emailed her back and she responded. I think that is wonderful. I think customer service is a huge part of it as well and Bonnie was fantastic! From getting the tickets to after we took the tour.

If you're looking for a tour to hear true stories and capturing great photos with many orbs and such I think this is a great choice. I read the reviews in researching my options for ghost tours in Williamsburg and spooks and legends were number 1. And from the ones I did read Bonnie replied to every one. That also was a huge plus for me. I also loved how Bonnie dressed in the time period and had her character and didn't break her character until the tour was done. There were other tours going on at the time. As one walked by before ours started it was a guy leading it in no costume and sounded just like a history story that you would hear on your day tours in Williamsburg. My husband and I enjoyed this tour and I would recommend it. We are from Maine but, if we ever go back I would love to take it again. Thank you again Bonnie for a great experience!

Visited September 2013
Bodoinham, ME

"Loved it!"

My husband and I went on the tour October 19th and we had a wonderful time! The guide was entertaining and informative. She made the stories of all of the places we visited come alive! We saw other tours while we were out and I was glad we took this tour. Other tour guides did not respect the homes and other people around them. We will take the tour again!

Visited October 2013
Hampton, VA

"A little rain didn't dull this tour."

Even though it rained the night of our tour, it was still a fun tour. Thoroughly enjoyed it! The narration that guided us was entertaining, which made it even more enjoyable. I hate tours with boring tour guides, this was far from that!

Visited October 2013
Melmass79

"Bonnie is "Spooktacular""

This was my third haunted tour in Williamsburg and by far the best. I was hesitant about another haunted tour of Williamsburg because the last one (Ax Wild Yours) was so horrible. Finding the group was a little difficult because there was a huge concert going on in Merchants Square so they were not in front of the cheese shop. A little common sense told me to check the other sides of the shop and there they were. Bonnie's knowledge, characterization and respect for the sites surpassed my expectations. She not only provided a tour but wanted her "guests" to experience as much as humanly...or hauntingly possible. I would tour again with her just to experience more.

Visited October 2013
New York City, NY

www.ingramcontent.com/pod-product-compliance
Lightning Source LLC
Chambersburg PA
CBHW070156290526
45789CB00002B/791